Contents

What foods should I eat?

 Your body needs a balance of different kinds of foods to grow and be healthy. There are five main food groups.

1. Bread, potatoes, breakfast cereals and other cereals, like pasta, maize, rice and oats. Also beans and *pulses*

2. Fruit and vegetables

3. Milk and *dairy foods*

4. Meat, fish and alternatives, like beans and pulses, nuts and eggs

5. Foods with fat and sugar, like biscuits, crisps, cakes, butter, jam and ice cream

Which food groups can you see here?
(Answer on page 23)

Foods from the first group should be the main part of your *diet*. Fill yourself up with cereals. Eat plenty of crispy, crunchy fruit and vegetables too. Your body needs less dairy foods and meat.

It's fine to eat foods like crisps and cake now and again. Watch you don't fill up on them though. It's fun to try out different foods from all the food groups.

What foods give you energy?

Food like bread, breakfast cereals, potatoes, pasta and rice give you energy that lasts. When you are playing sports, these will keep you going until the end of the game.

Wholemeal bread and *wholegrain* rice and pasta are better for you than the white kinds. They're tasty too.

A jacket potato with cheese makes a delicious energy food.

What do you spread on your bread? Be careful not to use too much butter or margarine.

The way we prepare energy food is important. Try not to eat fried food like chips too often.

Do you ever get hungry between meals? Pack a healthy snack to give you energy fast. Have an apple, banana or some raisins.

Why are fruit and veg healthy?

Fruit and vegetables give you **vitamins**. Vitamins help your body to work properly and fight *infection*.

There are many kinds of vegetables to choose from. Have you tried baby peas or sweetcorn? You can eat some vegetables raw. Others have to be cooked.

Fruit is fantastic. Do you enjoy juicy pears and crunchy apples? Oranges are delicious and sweet.

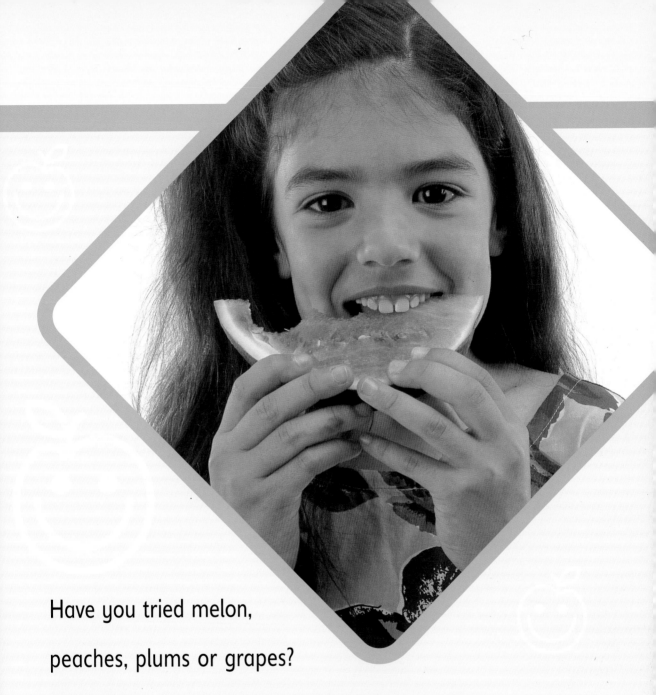

Have you tried melon,

peaches, plums or grapes?

Remember that fruit juice is good for you too.

Do you eat at least five kinds of fruit and vegetables each day? That's what your body needs.

Do I have to drink milk?

 It's good to drink milk. Milk and *dairy* foods like cheese and yoghurt help you to grow. They make your bones and teeth strong and healthy.

For breakfast, enjoy a big bowl of breakfast cereal with milk. It gives you lots of energy. Go for cereal sweetened with fruit rather than sugar.

Yoghurt is a tasty, healthy snack. Which flavours have you tried?

Cheese and yoghurt are good for you too. Children's yoghurts sometimes have a lot of added sugar though. Check the *ingredients* on a pot of yoghurt. Does it have sugar in it? Try making your own fruit yoghurt. Add your favourite fruit to natural yoghurt. It's healthier without added sugar.

Are meat and fish good for me?

Meat and fish are *protein* foods. They help you to grow and stay healthy. Protein foods have vitamins too.

Meat is a great way to get protein. You need to be careful though. Some meaty foods, such as sausages and bacon, are full of fat. Eat them only occasionally. Chicken and *lean* meat are better for you.

Fish makes a tasty dish. Try some different kinds.

Oily fish like mackerel,

salmon and

sardines are

very good

for you.

Fish is

better

without batter.

Fried fish is fatty.

It's best not to visit the fish and chip shop too often.

Why can't I eat crisps every day?

Think of all your favourite party foods. Are some of them on these lists?

Sugary foods:

fizzy drinks, sweets,

jam, puddings,

cakes, biscuits

Fatty foods:

chocolate, cake, crisps,

biscuits, ice cream,

butter, cream

It's fine to eat these things at a party, because you don't go to parties every day.

Eating fatty and sugary foods every day would be bad for you. Many of these foods have lots of salt too. Too much fat and salt are bad for your heart. Sugar can rot your beautiful teeth.

It's sensible to eat just a few sweet treats, now and again.

What's wrong with fizzy drinks?

 Most fizzy drinks are full of sugar. We all know sugar is bad for our teeth.

It's OK to have a fizzy drink with your meal once in a while. If you drink sugary drinks between meals, though, the sugar stays on your teeth. It can lead to **tooth decay**.

How many times do you clean your teeth each day? You should clean them twice a day.

When you're thirsty, pour yourself some fresh water.

Mix water with different kinds of fruit juice for a

change. Milk is healthy too. Why not make a milkshake?

What if I'm vegetarian?

Everyone needs to eat protein. You can get protein from plenty of foods, not just meat and fish. **Vegetarians** need to choose several of these delicious foods as part of a balanced diet. Then they will have no problem getting enough protein.

Enjoy a boiled egg or try some **tofu**. Go nutty for nuts and tasty seeds. Stir them into pasta or place them on pizzas.

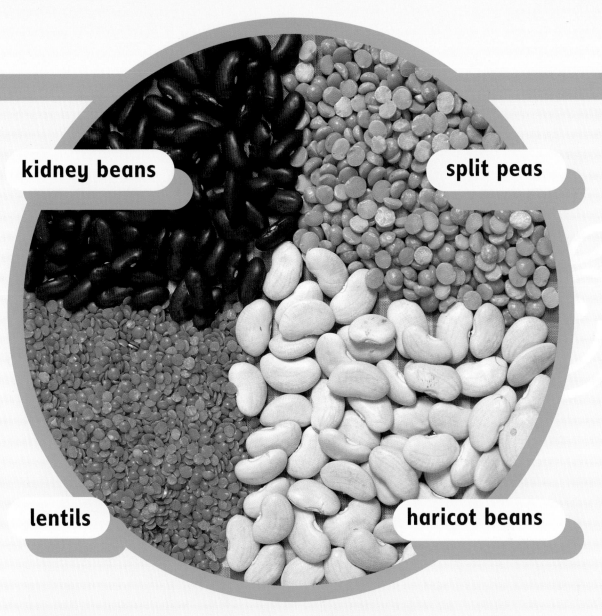

kidney beans

split peas

lentils

haricot beans

Be full of beans – and other *pulses*. Pulses are the seeds of vegetable plants. They come in all shapes, sizes and colours. You'll find them in soups and salads, pies and curries.

What are special diets?

 Some people can't eat certain foods because they make them feel very ill. You might know someone who is **allergic** to nuts.

Other people avoid certain foods because of their beliefs. Muslims and Jewish people don't eat meat from a pig. Hindus will not eat beef. Vegetarians do not eat meat or fish because they don't want to harm animals.

This Jewish boy is enjoying a pitta bread snack that contains no meat from a pig.

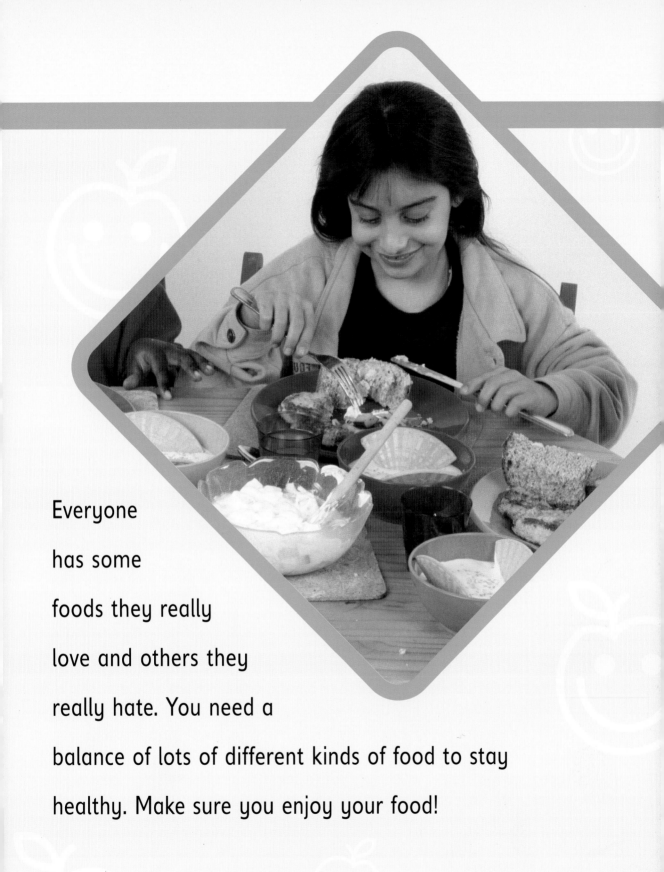

Everyone

has some

foods they really

love and others they

really hate. You need a

balance of lots of different kinds of food to stay

healthy. Make sure you enjoy your food!

Glossary and index

tooth decay	16	When a tooth begins to rot, leaving a hole that needs to be filled.
vegetarians	18	People who do not eat meat or fish.
vitamins	8	Natural substances found in different foods. They help people to grow and stay healthy.
wholegrain	6	Made with all the grain of a cereal, with nothing taken out.
wholemeal	6	Made with whole grains of wheat.

Answer to question:

P.4 The food groups in the picture are from groups 1, 2, and 4.

Finding out more

Books to read:

Eat Well (Safe and Sound)
by Angela Royston
(Heinemann Library, 2000)

Why Should I Eat Well?
by Claire Llewellyn and Mike Gordon
(Hodder Wayland, 2001)